RAILWAY
• HALSGROVE •
SERIES

YORKSHIRE HERITAGE STEAM RAILWAYS

Mike and Karl Heath

HALSGROVE

First published in Great Britain in 2016

British Library Cataloguing-in-Publication Data
A CIP record for this title is available from the
British Library

ISBN 978 0 85704 261 3

HALSGROVE
Halsgrove House,
Ryelands Business Park,
Bagley Road, Wellington, Somerset TA21 9PZ
Tel: 01823 653777   Fax: 01823 216796
email: sales@halsgrove.com

Part of the Halsgrove group of companies
Information on all Halsgrove titles is available at:
www.halsgrove.com

Printed and bound in China by
Everbest Printing Investment Ltd

CONTENTS

INTRODUCTION

The historic county of Yorkshire, the largest in the United Kingdom is a vast and varied region. With a population greater than that of Wales concentrated in the south of the county, the vast area to the north forms one of the most sparsely populated corners of the nation. It also has some of the best steam and heritage railways in the country.

South Yorkshire sat at the heart of the industrial revolution in England. From medieval times the use of locally mined coal and iron gave rise to important industries from steelwork to textiles. In the associated heyday of the railways, Leeds became a major hub for the meeting of lines boasting more junctions than York and Crewe combined. It is no surprise that it also became a centre for locomotive manufacture and at its peak, no other city in the British Isles had more builders within its boundaries. Only the Hunslet Engine Company survives but the area does retain 'the oldest continually working public railway in the world'. Founded in 1758, the Middleton Railway was the first railway in the world to use revenue-earning steam locomotives in 1812 and also the first standard gauge railway to be taken over by volunteers in 1960. Operated entirely by volunteers, train services now run between Moor Road Station and Middleton Park in South Leeds.

The north-west of the county is taken over by the enchanting scenery of the Yorkshire Dales National Park, characterised by spectacular limestone valleys with upland pastures separated by dry-stone walls and grazed by sheep and cattle. Add to this a scattering of picture postcard villages and historic castles and abbeys and it is easy to see why the area boasts being 'a place that stirs the emotions and stimulates the senses of everyone that visits'. Just outside the charming market town of Skipton, 'the Gateway to the Dales' is Embsay, home of the Embsay & Bolton Abbey Steam Railway. Marketed as Yorkshire's friendly line, it has one of the finest collections of ex-industrial tank locomotives and working examples operate services between Embsay and Bolton Abbey where passengers can alight and visit the nearby ruins of the twelfth century Augustinian monastery.

Nestling on the mid-western border with Lancashire are the Brontë Moors, a windswept area of heather and wild moor covering predominantly millstone grit that has created crags and scenery that generate an air of bleakness depicted so vividly in the classic works of the Brontë sisters, Charlotte, Emily and Anne. On the edge of the moors lies the village of Haworth, the base for the Keighley & Worth Valley Railway which runs like a ribbon for 5 miles through Brontë Country from the industrial town of Keighley through Oakworth and Haworth to the terminus at Oxenhope. The journey, travels through some of the most famous and exhilarating scenery in the world, none more so than the station at Oakworth which was the focal point for Lionel Jeffries' film version of E. Nesbit's book *The Railway Children*.

To the north-east are the North Yorkshire Moors. This breathtaking region is home to spectacular heather moorland, pine forests, rolling hills and a rugged coastline. Travelling through the heart of this National Park from Pickering to Grosmont and on to the coastal town of Whitby, is the North Yorkshire Moors Railway. This line is a major tourist attraction and the olde world charm of the line's country stations together with the remote unspoilt scenery has provided locations for much television and film work, notably for the first Harry Potter film, when Goathland Station took on the guise of Hogsmeade Station.

Away from the heritage lines, one of the most famous sections of the national rail network also passes through Yorkshire. The Settle to Carlisle Railway runs through the most remote scenic regions of the Yorkshire Dales from its junction with the Leeds to Morecambe line just south of the town of Settle, through Horton-in-Ribblesdale on to

Ribblehead and over the famous Ribblehead Viaduct before crossing the boundary into Cumbria and onward to Carlisle. Throughout the year private operators run steam hauled railtours that travel the line giving passengers unrivalled views across the Pennine hills.

What follows is a photographic journey along each of the railways mentioned depicting all aspects of steam railway preservation, the restored locomotives and rolling stock that operate on the lines and the rich and varied landscapes through which they pass. We hope you enjoy the trip!

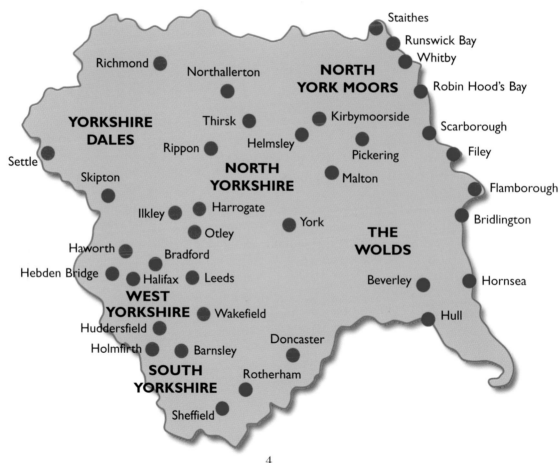

The Middleton Railway

The area around Middleton saw coal mining from as early as the thirteenth century and the colliery railway itself secured its place in history by nature of the then land and coal owner, Charles Brandling, obtaining an Act of Parliament securing the route of his waggonway. This was the very first Act in respect of the building of a waggonway or railway.

From 1758 coal was transported down to Leeds and the availability of this cheap fuel saw Leeds develop a multitude of industries including metal-working, brick, glass and pottery manufacture and cloth making in steam-powered mills.

Initially horses provided the motive power until 1812 when the railway became the first in the world to successfully employ steam locomotives commercially. Steam traction was introduced operating on a rack and pinion system where each of four locomotives, locally built for the purpose, had a large rack wheel at one side that engaged with cogs cast in to the rails. These locomotives worked the line until the last one literally became worn out in 1835. At this point horses returned to bear the burden.

Meanwhile the experience gained in locomotive design and construction and the growth of steam railways generally saw Leeds develop as a major locomotive manufacturing centre. Steam returned to the railway in 1866, with Manning Wardle locomotives, and the track was upgraded to the 'standard gauge' (4 feet 8 ½ inches) in 1881.

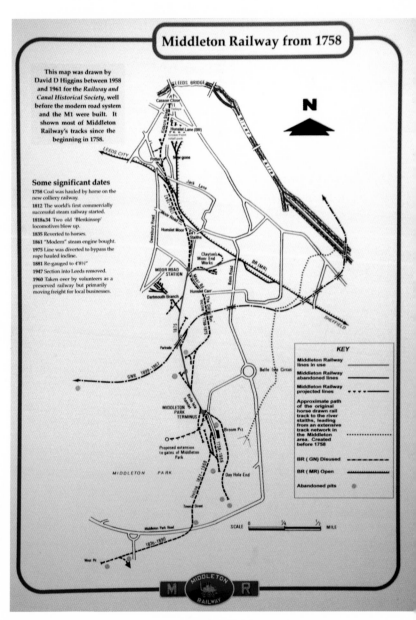

Middleton Railway from 1758

This map was drawn by David D Higgins between 1958 and 1961 for the *Railway and Canal Historical Society*, well before the modern road system and the M1 were built. It shown most of Middleton Railway's tracks since the beginning in 1758.

Some significant dates

1758 Coal was hauled by horse on the new colliery railway.
1812 The world's first commercially successful steam railway started.
1818&34 Two old 'Blenkinsop' locomotives blow up.
1835 Reverted to horses.
1861 "Modern" steam engine bought.
1975 Line was diverted to bypass the rope hauled incline.
1881 Re-gauged to 4'8½".
1947 Section into Leeds removed.
1960 Taken over by volunteers as a preserved railway but primarily moving freight for local businesses.

MAPS & LOGO REPRODUCED WITH KIND PERMISSION OF THE MIDDLETON RAILWAY SOCIETY

5

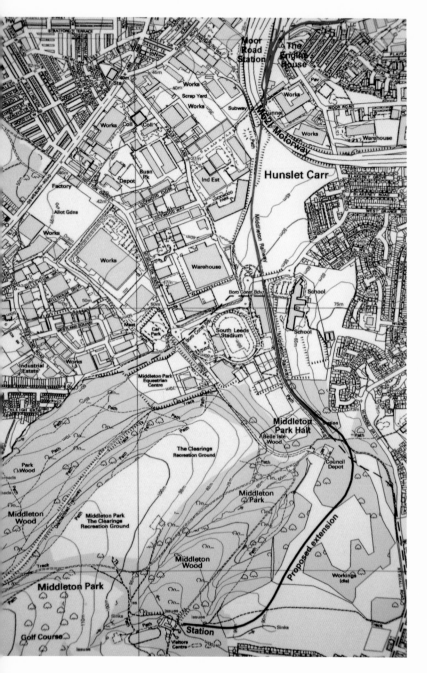

For many years the railway faithfully served the ever-increasing industrial demands of Leeds until the line was substantially rationalised as the collieries were nationalised in 1947.

During the fifties coal traffic had declined to such an extent that in 1960 the National Coal Board sold part of the railway to a neighbouring company, Clayton, Son & Company. They allowed a group of enthusiasts from Leeds University to move their small collection, initially trams, onto an abandoned section of track between Moor Road and the connection to the former Great Northern Railway line. The group, soon to be named the Middleton Railway Trust, not only began to hold open days but were also employed by Claytons to run goods traffic for them and this continued until 1983. It was then that the goods traffic stopped and Claytons closed down their Dartmouth Works site, where the society had thus far been based.

A new home was found at the current Moor Road site, and new tracks were laid to accommodate their, by now, substantial collections and a workshop and combined ticket office and shop constructed.

Alterations to the site culminated in the new Engine House, incorporating a shop, museum and display hall, being opened by Sir William McAlpine on 14 April 2007. Today the railway runs from Moor Road Station to Park Halt on the northern edge of Middleton Park where evidence of the early mining can still be found.

THE MIDDLETON RAILWAY

Began nearby in 1758 to carry coal from Middleton Colliery to Leeds by horse-drawn wagon. The world's first commercially successful steam locomotives, designed and built by Matthew Murray and incorporating John Blenkinsop's patented rack wheel, started work here on 24 June 1812.

The Engine House includes a splendid museum that tells the story of not just the colliery railway but also the local locomotive industry and is where a fine collection of Leeds-built railway locomotives, both steam and diesel, can be viewed at close quarters.

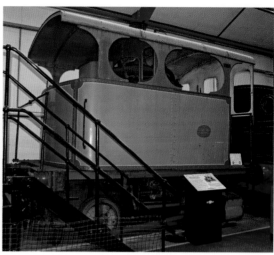

The exhibits also include some foreign traction and this odd-looking 0-4-0 shunting locomotive heralds from Belgium. Cockeril No. 1625 'Lucie' was built in Liege in 1890. It arrived at the railway in 1995 and until withdrawal in December 2000 was the oldest locomotive in the operating fleet. At the 1997 Gala it was operating services in tandem with the Hunslet diesel 'John Alcock' that dates from 1932.

The other continental locomotive on display is a 0-4-0WT No. 385 built in 1895 by the German company of Richard Hartmann. Used by the Danish State Railway to shunt stock on and off the ferries that serviced the many islands around Denmark it arrived at Middleton in 1972. At that same 1997 Gala it was paired with British 'well tank' locomotive, 'Bellerophon', which is a 0-6-0WT built at the Haydock Foundry in 1874, for use at their collieries. The pair have just emerged from beneath the M621 motorway and are passing the Dartmouth branch junction. No. 385 is currently awaiting overhaul.

Another locomotive operating at that 1997 Gala and now in the overhaul queue is 'Mirvale' a relative youngster being built by Hunslet in 1955. After working at the Mirvale Chemical Company until 1964, in 1968 it moved into preservation at the North Yorkshire Moors Railway gaining celebrity status as the first locomotive to traverse the full length of the preserved line between Grosmont and Pickering. However in reality it was too small for regular work on that line so languished behind the scenes there until put up for sale in 1986. The Middleton Railway Trust and a number of individual members got together and successfully bid for 'Mirvale' bringing it back to Leeds in December 1986. After restoration it entered service in 1990 and worked up to 1998 when it was withdrawn for boiler repairs.

One of the oldest locomotives at Middleton is North Eastern Railway 0-4-0T No. 1310 which was built in 1891, for dock shunting and departmental duties, at that railway's Gateshead works. In 1931 it was sold to the Pelaw Main Collieries with ownership transferring to the National Coal Board on Nationalisation in 1947. After moving around a number of Colliery Railways 1310's scrapyard destiny in 1964, was avoided when another group of enthusiasts banded together to form the Steam Power Trust 65 and purchase the locomotive. In 1965 it arrived at Middleton and was restored to full NER livery. This is one locomotive that was operating back in 1997 and is fully operational today, having undergone a boiler overhaul in the intervening years.

Manning, Wardle and Co. 0-6-0T No. 1210 'Sir Berkeley', built 1890, is another locomotive photographed back in 1997 and in service at the present time. After an uneventful life working around a number of collieries the locomotive was purchased by an individual and transferred to the Keighley & Worth Valley Railway in 1965. In the early 1980s ownership was transferred to the Vintage Carriages Trust, now based at Ingrow on the KWVR, and after restoration 'Sir Berkeley' entered active service in 1991. After a period of travelling around many preserved railways, including a visit to mainland Europe, it became based at Middleton and was a regular performer until expiry of its boiler ticket in 2001. Restoration work between 2004 and 2007 saw the locomotive return to full working order. During overhaul its boiler was found to be beyond economic repair but rather than just scrap it the Society imaginatively cut sections out to show visitors just how a locomotive boiler works. A new boiler was built for the loco.

These last two photographs from 1997 are of a freight train 'top and tailed' by 'Sir Berkeley' and No. 1310 on the remains of the Dartmouth Branch line that once linked various metal industries with the 'main' line. At that Gala enthusiasts were able to ride in the guards van affording the opportunity to traverse this very rarely used section of track since the society vacated the Dartmouth Works site.

As part of the site redevelopment for the Engine House in 2006 Moor Road Station was re-constructed as a single platform with waiting shelter for passengers and coaling and watering facilities for the locomotives.

Hudswell Clarke 0-6-0ST 'Slough Estates No. 3' is about to depart Moor Road. This locomotive was built in 1924 and remained in service at the Slough Trading Estates in Buckinghamshire until closure in 1973. After a period spent at the Mid-Hants Railway ownership transferred to the Slough & Windsor Railway Society who steadily progressed restoration work. An enforced move saw the locomotive arrive at the Swindon & Cricklade Railway in Wiltshire where the benefit of a covered workshop saw the restoration completed and the locomotive returned to steam in 2000. Further works to the boiler were required in 2009. It arrived at Middleton on long term loan in 2011.

The line runs for 1¼ miles to Park Halt on the northern edge of Middleton Park, which is described as the green jewel of South Leeds. The park is a mixture of traditional parkland and ancient woodland and in addition to providing evidence of early mining activity has much to occupy visitors of all ages, including a café, bowling greens, a playground and fishing lake.

The industrial history of the line attracts much interest from photographers wishing to recreate scenes from the past. One such event in September 2010 was organised by Martin Creese's 30742 Charters Group which saw two Hudswell, Clarke-built Manchester Ship Canal locomotives in operation on the branch. No. 32 'Gothenburg' was built in 1903 and is usually to be found on the East Lancashire Railway, Bury in the guise of Thomas the Tank Engine.

These photographs show the short freight working departing Moor Road, and emerging from the tunnel beneath the M621 motorway.

The other former Manchester Ship Canal locomotive in operation was Middleton's own No. 67 which is a later version, dating from 1919 and constructed with longer water tanks. No. 67 spent all its working life on the MSC system which was the largest privately owned railway system in the world. In 1969 it was privately purchased and moved to the then infant Keighley & Worth Valley Railway. Whilst it worked some of the lighter duties on that line, it was in reality underpowered for everyday use and moved to Middleton in October 1995. A 1927 built Wallis & Steevens road roller completed the scene as the train turned the clocks back by travelling along the Balm Road Branch.

The day included a number of cameo recreations set up on and alongside the disused Dartmouth Branch.

The Middleton Railway may not be the longest of preserved lines but its historical significance cannot be underestimated. The twenty-first century backdrop to this photograph owes its very existence to the mining and railway heritage that the Middleton Railway Trust has preserved for the benefit of generations present and future – it is well worth a visit.

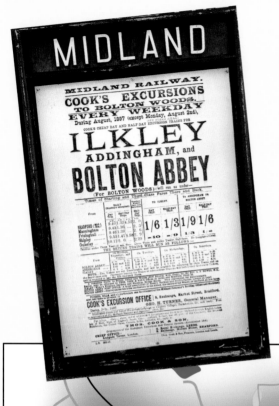

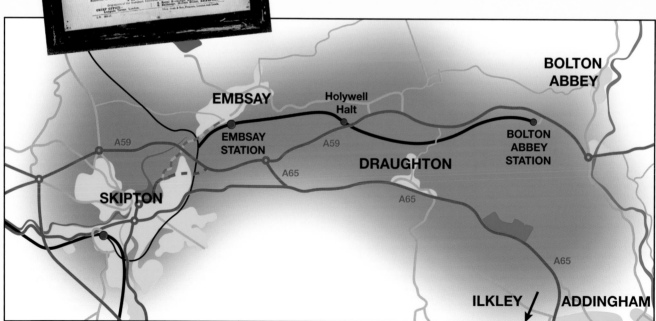

MAPS & LOGO REPRODUCED WITH KIND PERMISSION OF
THE EMBSAY & BOLTON ABBEY STEAM RAILWAY

The Embsay & Bolton Abbey Steam Railway

The Embsay & Bolton Abbey Steam Railway operates over a 4-mile stretch of the former trackbed of the Skipton & Ilkley Railway.

Skipton had been rail connected since September 1847 when the Leeds & Bradford (Shipley to Colne extension) Railway was extended from Keighley. Colne was reached the following year. In 1850 the through route from Skipton to Lancaster was established which also provided a link with the Lancaster and Carlisle Railway that was to become a part of the West Coast Line from London to Glasgow. This opened up access to Carlisle and Scotland to travellers from the West Riding.

It was August 1865 when the Otley & Ilkley Joint Railway arrived in Ilkley. This line connected the town with the Leeds & Thirsk Railway via Otley and Arthington. At that time Ilkley was a terminus.

Twenty years later in April 1885 a contract for the construction of the new Skipton & Ilkley Railway was awarded to a company from Bristol, Mousley & Co. On 16 May 1888 the line opened for passenger traffic between Ilkley and Bolton Abbey with Skipton reached a few months later. Until final closure in 1965 the line not only provided a local passenger and freight service but also became an important diversionary route whilst track repairs or accident blockages elsewhere were dealt with.

Just east of Embsay was the junction with the Skipton to Grassington and Threshfield Branch. This branch had not been closed but in the late sixties fears grew that it too was to succumb to this fate. At this time railway enthusiasts, buoyed by the success of the volunteers locally in reopening lines such as the Middleton Railway and Keighley & Worth Valley Railway, started to consider the possibility of the Grassington Branch becoming a preserved steam railway. To this end the Embsay & Grassington Railway Preservation Society was formed in 1968. However fears about this particular branch line's future proved unfounded as British Rail revealed that it was to be maintained as far as Swinden Quarry at Cracoe. Tilcon Ltd had taken over the works and were to commence running a regular flow of stone trains along it. The many fund raising activities undertaken by the society included the operation of special trains chartered from British Rail. In 1970 one such 'special' was the last train to Grassington just before the track between Grassington and Swinden was taken up.

With their plans now revised to the opening of a steam railway centre based around Embsay Station and the small section of track that remained, the Society changed its name to the Yorkshire Dales Railway Society to reflect this new proposal.

In 1970 the YDRS commenced the renting of Embsay Station giving them a base from which they could operate. When first formed back in 1968 the members had reached the conclusion that the most economic way of running and maintaining a fleet of steam locomotives was to use former industrial types. At the time these were readily available and would offer lower running costs than the ex-British Railways main line locos.

Their collection of suitable locomotives was growing and open days offering brake van rides commenced. Regular services continued right up to 1974 when a ban on all preserved railways operating on track leased from them was imposed by British Railways. With no other option but to obtain their own Light Railway Order they submitted an application to the Railway Inspectorate. An inspector duly arrived and provided them with a list of works that would have to be carried out before the Light Railway Order could be granted. The works required were extensive and included the construction of a run-round loop at the now named Bow Bridge Junction. It was not until May 1979 that the Railway was able to operate steam trains again. During those three years the Railway recruited working members who had to work tirelessly to both carry out the required works and raise the necessary funds without the benefit of income from an operating railway. The official opening of the Yorkshire Dales Railway took place on 19 May 1979 and the railway settled down with regular steam-hauled passenger services operating between Embsay and Bow Bridge Junction.

Around this time charitable status had been granted and the Yorkshire Dales Railway Museum Trust was set up to assist with the purchase of the freehold of the site.

The society now turned its attention to the disused trackbed leading to Bolton Abbey and its long term objective of 'Steam Trains to Bolton Abbey'.

The first stage took the line to Skibeden, one mile from Embsay, where a run-round loop was constructed. A little further beyond was the bridge that carried the A59 over the disused trackbed. Fears over its condition had led to the County Council reinforcing it by filling the cutting below. This obstacle to progress was overcome with assistance from the North Yorkshire County Council and Craven District Council. Reinforcement in the form of a steel tunnel was introduced under the bridge. Tracklaying was extended to Holywell Bridge where the society decided to introduce a typical rural halt, to be called Holywell Halt which opened in July 1987. With planning permission for a run-round loop at their next target destination, Draughton, refused, the next stage took the railway to Stoneacre. This section opened in 1991. The success of railway operations to Stoneacre gave impetus to the purchase of the remaining 2 miles of trackbed to Bolton Abbey. Further society name changes evolved to more accurately reflect the line's operations.

Preparatory works commenced and thirty years of undergrowth had to be cleared, culverts and drains renewed, fences repaired and three new bridges constructed. February 1997 saw the first work's train steam into Bolton Abbey Station. The official opening was held on 26 October 1997.

Bolton Abbey Station was completely rebuilt from a derelict collapsed shell, to the 1888 plans of the original. This was no mean feat and involved the assistance of many bodies. At the time Yorkshire Television had introduced a programme called 'Action Time' which included appeals for labour and materials to complete a particular project. The rebuilding of Bolton Abbey Station was one such project and the appeal quickly brought in a firm of architects who drew up the plans and specification. There were also many offers to supply materials and the complete electrical installation. The next requirement was a builder.

Step forward Sir Robert McAlpine who agreed to supervise and construct the new station. In all over 150 businesses contributed in one way or another to the rebuilding between 1995 and 1997.

A grand re-opening ceremony was held on 26 October 1997 with Sir Robert McAlpine as the guest of honour. Sir William McAlpine performed the official opening on 1 May 1998.

In its heyday the station had two platforms and a footbridge, but one of the platforms became redundant and the footbridge was dismantled after closure. The railway is currently appealing for funds to enable them to restore the second platform with long-term plans to return the whole location to how it would have looked during the Midland, LMS and British Railways era.

The station plays host to the Hambleton Valley 7 ¼ inch gauge Miniature Railway which operates on most days when trains are running. Its station is beside the Bolton Abbey Station lawn and the line travels a distance of 220 yards which includes a crossing over the station's main drive.

A popular date in the railway's events calendar is the 1940s' Weekend. The nostalgia of wartime Britain is relived with various re-enactment societies attending, creating depictions of the Home Guard at work as soldiers and airmen return home on leave. The platform scenes are complemented with field camps on the station lawn and vehicles of the period on the forecourt.

The signalbox was brought to the site from Guiseley Junction on the Ilkley line, whilst the water tower came from Skipton. On 19 December 2009, in appropriate weather conditions, a Santa Special departs hauled by Great Western Railway 0-6-2T No. 5643. This locomotive, built in 1925, is owned by the Furness Railway Trust and is usually based at the Ribble Steam Railway in Preston.

Another 0-6-2 GWR Tank locomotive to visit the line was No. 6619. This was built in 1928 and is currently based on the Kent & East Sussex Railway. This locomotive spent much of the summer of 2011 in Yorkshire.

The mainstay of the railway's motive power remains industrial tank locomotives. On 5 April 2015 'Beatrice' piloted 'Norman' on an afternoon service. 'Beatrice' was built by Hunslet in Leeds in 1945 and worked at the Acton Hall Colliery, Pontefract. 'Norman' is a Robert Stephenson and Hawthorns-built Austerity (1943) that had worked at Askern Colliery, Doncaster. It arrived on the line, midway through an overhaul and is owned by Southern Locomotives Ltd who are based at Swanage on the south coast. It entered service in time for the main 2011 running season. The absence of the dome cover in the picture indicates that it was on test following some winter maintenance work.

In this telephoto view taken in November 2013, from the edge of the village of Draughton, the train is emerging from the woods that surround Hambleton Quarry, an old limestone quarry which in the early 1900s had standard gauge sidings from a junction at the Ilkley end of Bolton Abbey Station. The quarry closed in 1921.

5 December 2010, the Dales are carpeted with snow and 0-6-0ST 'Darfield' is in charge of the 'Santa' trains. 'Darfield' is another product of the Hunslet Engine Company, Leeds dating from 1953 and is named after the colliery where it spent most of its working life. It initially arrived at Embsay in December 1975, restoration work took five years and the locomotive entered service in early 1981. At that time services were operating between Embsay and Holywell Halt. More work to the boiler was required following withdrawal in 1983 after which it ran up until the end of 1987. The following year the locomotive was moved to the Llangollen Railway but returned as a visitor in June 2008 and stayed until the end of the 'Santa' season in 2010.

Opposite: In May 2007 there were bluebells aplenty as No. 140 passes by. This PLA type 0-6-0T locomotive was built by Hudswell Clarke in 1948. (A major customer of Hudswell Clarke was the Port of London Authority and this association spawned a standard design of locomotive that would become known as the PLA type). Before coming to the railway it worked at NCB's Horden Colliery, County Durham. This locomotive is currently out of service awaiting overhaul.

Demonstration freight trains are a feature of 'Branch-Line' weekends when all available motive power is put to work. In May 2014 'Norman' is seen approaching Draughton with a mixed goods train.

Two years earlier 'Norman' in a dark green livery was captured heading for Bolton Abbey with some stone hoppers.

34

A truly vintage workhorse is just about to pass under the Priors Lane road bridge on a lovely summer's day in July 2014.
Carrying its LMS livery, No. 12322 is the Lancashire & Yorkshire 'A' Class 0-6-0 (No. 1300) that was built at the L&Y
works in Horwich in 1895. Whilst periodically based at Embsay it does visit other preserved railways from time to time.

Stoneacre loop viewed from the hilltop fields off Low Lane, Draughton. The line from Embsay to here opened in 1991 and this served as the extent of the journey until Bolton Abbey Station was reached in 1997. Following the re-opening to Bolton Abbey the loop was fully equipped with semaphore signalling and the railway constructed a new brick-built signalbox. The remnants of steam in the distance indicates that the Embsay-bound train departed the loop before No. 140 was allowed to continue on its way.

A hard frost welcomed the first 'Santa' trains of the 2008 season. The signal has been raised allowing 'Darfield' entry to the loop.

5 December 2010 was a superb day for steam railway photography. Sun, snow and bitingly low temperatures – ideal for crisp, creamy exhaust trails. 'Darfield' duly obliges as it powers away from Stoneacre.

A winter weather comparison – Above: Another shot of 'Darfield' on that winter's day in 2010. Below: GWR 0-6-2 Tank No. 6619 almost exactly one year later. This 56xx 'Taffy' Tank class was designed for work hauling heavy coal trains in the valleys of South Wales. 6619 had spent its preserved life on the North Yorkshire Moors Railway until its owners put it up for sale and moved it to Embsay whilst a purchaser was sought. It was subsequently sold to the Kent & East Sussex Railway.

A frosty panoramic view towards Holywell Halt as seen from the hill behind the signalbox at Stoneacre.

Pannier Tank No. 6435, a visitor from the Bodmin & Wenford Railway in Cornwall, is getting into its stride between Stoneacre and Holywell Halt. This is a popular location for photography with locomotives having to work on the climb out of the loop.

When 'Taffy' Tank No. 6619 was bought by the Kent & East Sussex Railway and arrangements made to transport the locomotive south, to fill the temporary void in Embsay's running fleet, the K&ESR sent USA 0-6-0 tank No. 65 for a short period at the back end of 2012. These 1942-3 built ex-United States Army Transportation Corps S100 Class locomotives were purchased and adapted by the Southern Railway after the end of the Second World War to replace the old London & South Western Railway B4 class that worked the docks at Southampton.

Early spring 2015 with 'Beatrice' in charge of services.

In March 2013 'Norman' was still carrying its green livery. Later that same year, for the railway's 125th Anniversary Weekend, it would be painted black as a pseudo British Railways locomotive No. 68005. (See earlier photograph of 'Norman' on a freight train approaching Draughton.) The train is about to pass under the A59 road bridge by Holywell Halt.

The profile of the steel tunnel type reinforcement built under the A59 road bridge, to support it, is clearly visible in this photograph of No. 22 approaching Holywell Halt.

'Darfield' passes in spring 2010. The area is significant geologically and the cutting at Holywell Bridge is designated a 'Site of Scientific Interest' as it provides exposures of the lowest beds of the carboniferous limestone visible in the Craven District. There is a viewing platform at the top of the cutting.

Holywell Halt was the first extension on the railway with the line from Embsay opening in July 1987. The Society constructed a typical rural halt here, with a single platform and shelter. An area of woodland on either side of the track was acquired and opened up to provide a recreational picnic area.

Another Hunslet-built Austerity Class 0-6-0ST arrived for a flying visit in August 2010. No.22 was built in Leeds in 1956 for the NCB Graig Merthyr Colliery in South Wales. Its preservation base is the Nene Valley Railway near Peterborough.

The railway achieved a preservation coup in 2008 when LNER Class D49/1 4-4-0 No. 246 'Morayshire' paid its first ever visit to a preserved railway in England. Built at Darlington in 1928, its working life was spent in Scotland right up to withdrawal in 1961. It is usually to be found at the Bo'ness & Kinneil Railway near Grangemouth.

On 21 September 2008 'Morayshire' was hauling vintage coaches from the 'Stately Trains' collection. Immediately behind the locomotive is Great Eastern Railway No.14, a 6-wheeler built in Stratford in 1889. At the rear of the train is another GER coach. No. 8 was built as a Third Class Family Saloon in 1877, but is thought to have been the private saloon of Princess Alice as features not usually associated with third class accommodation were revealed during restoration. Sandwiched between was ex-Great North of Scotland Railway No. 34, a 1st/3rd 6-wheeled carriage that dates from 1896.

Another wonderful Christmas card scene from December 2010 with 'Darfield' working the 'Santa Special' away from the sidings at Skibeden on the approach to the footbridge close to Holywell Halt.

Embsay Station originally opened in 1888 and was the first station on the Skipton to Ilkley line located at a point 2 miles from Skipton Station north junction. It survived right up to 22 March 1965 when the line, like so many others, succumbed to the Beeching axe. The preservation society took possession, initially on a rental basis, of the buildings in 1970 since when the site has developed including the addition of a waiting room which was a former cabman's shelter at Ilkley and a ticket office which was recovered from Barmouth Station.

49

A portrait of LNER No. 246 'Morayshire' arriving at Embsay with another vintage train on 21 September 2008.

No. 22 stands at the platform on a lovely sunny August day back in 2010.

On 20 September 2008 'Monkton No. 1' passes through with a demonstration freight train. This locomotive, a 1953 product of Hunslet in Leeds, was one of the later Austerity tanks. It was delivered new to the colliery of the same name at Royston near Barnsley. Closure of that mine in 1967 saw 'Monkton' transferred to North Gawber Colliery where it remained until 23 February 1980 which was the day it left the NCB for a new life at Embsay.

The railway has long-term ambitions to extend south-west back into Skipton itself but for now the line ends just short of the junction with the remaining active section of the former Grassington Branch.

As previously mentioned, for many years the E&BASR was marketed as Yorkshire's 'Friendly Line'. That ethos remains and an atmosphere of the rural branch line prevails, operated by industrial locomotives many of which were 'born and bred' in Yorkshire.

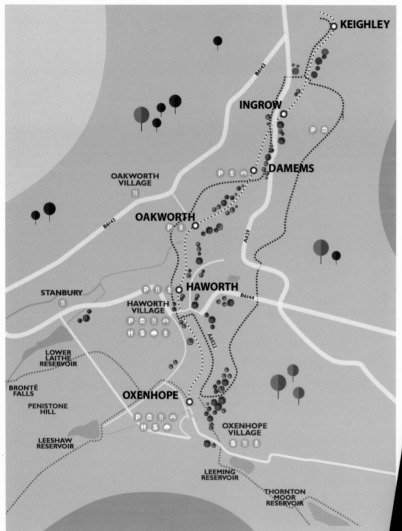

Keighley & Worth Valley Railway

MAP & LOGO REPRODUCED WITH KIND PERMISSION OF
THE KEIGHLEY & WORTH VALLEY RAILWAY

The Keighley & Worth Valley Railway

The Keighley & Worth Valley Railway is a 5 ½ mile branch line that was built to serve the mills and villages along the route and has notably been preserved in its entirety. From a junction with the national rail network at Keighley it winds its way up the valley of the River Worth through Ingrow and Damems to Oakworth. From here it leaves the River Worth to follow the course of Bridgehouse Beck passing by Haworth and on to the line's terminus at Oxenhope.

Funded by local mill owners, the first sod was cut in 1864 and three years later on 15 April 1867 the line opened. Operations soon became the responsibility of the Midland Railway Company that was incorporated into the London, Midland and Scottish Railway as part of the 1924 'Grouping' with Nationalisation in 1948 transferring ownership to the then newly-formed British Railways. The line continued to operate passenger services until 1961 with freight traffic surviving a further twelve months until final closure in 1962.

For over ninety-five years the steep gradient of the line had challenged locomotives of all sizes as they strove to transport passengers to and from work, and ship in hundreds of tons of coal to the mills to keep the steam-powered looms working.

Whilst many of the woollen mills had long since disappeared and road transport had attracted travellers away from the railways, there was a group of people that were not prepared for 1962 to be the last time that the sound of a steam locomotive tackling the climb would echo off the valley sides.

Local people and enthusiasts opposed to the closure worked extremely hard to create a preservation society that was ultimately to form a company that would purchase the line outright, lease access into Keighley Station and operate a regular public service.

It must be noted that by the time the preservation society took over the line, British Rail had left it to rot away with open access to vandals. It therefore took six years of hard graft by the volunteers before the line re-opened in 1968. Since then the line has gone from strength to strength developing into one of the country's premier heritage railways serving both the communities along the valley and attracting thousands of visitors each year to the beautiful countryside immortalised by Charlotte, Emily and Anne Brontë.

Keighley Station – the KWVR services operate out of Platforms 3 and 4 of what is a four platform station. Platforms 1 and 2 serve the national network's services westward through Skipton and to the east those via Leeds and Bradford. The station retains many original features such as the magnificent glass canopy supported on ornate cast ironwork, original waiting room and toilet facilities. 'Period' extras added include the ticket office, a former tobacco kiosk rescued from Manchester's old Central Station and a ticket collector's hut created from a telephone box that once stood at Wakefield Station.

On 7 March 2014 the station played host to a photography evening featuring the railway's WD Austerity 2-8-0 locomotive No. 90733 at the head of a freight train. On this occasion the smoke box number had been changed to 90711 which was the number from a locomotive that had operated locally out of Low Moor Shed in Bradford.

Top: *The climb out of Keighley is challenging for the locomotives and their crew with a tight curve and a gradient of 1 in 58 to contend with.*

London, Midland and Scottish Railway Ivatt Class 2MT No. 41241 tackles the climb on a sunny April afternoon in 2007. This locomotive was built in Crewe in 1949 and when new spent several years working along the famous Somerset and Dorset Railway being based at Bath (Green Park) Shed. It was well travelled by the time it was withdrawn from service at Skipton. Initially bought by two pioneering members of the society (ownership passed to the KWVR in 1970) it arrived on the railway in 1967.

Bottom: *20 September 2009 and the cobbled Low Mill Lane is unusually quiet as the railway's LMS Class 3F 'Jinty' 0-6-0 Tank No. 47279 heads south. 47279 dates from 1924 having been built by the Vulcan Foundry in St Helens. It was withdrawn and sold to Woodham Bros. Scrapyard in South Wales in 1967 where it languished until purchased in 1979 by a private group for use on the KWVR.*

In February 2010 ex-Great Northern Railway Class N2 0-6-2 Tank No. 1744, built in 1921 and usually based at the Great Central Railway in Loughborough visited the Yorkshire line and was captured approaching the top of Keighley Bank. The first two carriages in the train are also of Great Northern Railway vintage. The first is a six-wheeled Brake Third that was built in 1888 whilst the second is a Lavatory Composite Brake carriage which is ten years younger dating from 1898. They are part of the Vintage Carriages Trust collection.

The locomotive had been based on the KWVR in the early days of preservation and even had a supporting role in the original 'Railway Children' film in which it was seen speeding the 'Scotch Flyer' through Oakworth Station!

The top of Keighley Bank viewed from Longcroft with the Park Lane road bridge over the River Worth in the foreground. The whole scene a reminder of times gone by when mills were a common sight along the valley.

Hauling this 'Gala' day box van freight train, is Midland Railway Class 4F 0-6-0 No. 43924. Built at Derby in 1920 the locomotive spent its latter years around Gloucester and Bristol before it too ended up in the scrapyard at Barry in 1965. It arrived in Haworth in the summer of 1970 being the first of over 200 locomotives to be rescued from that South Wales yard.

On Gala weekends and selected summer Sundays the railway operates vintage trains using carriages from either its own collection or from that of the Vintage Carriages Trust at Ingrow. During the Gala in March 2013 a couple of Lancashire and Yorkshire Railway coaches formed the train that was hauled by the Bahamas Locomotive Society's 0-6-0 side tank 'Nunlow'. This locomotive heralds from Yorkshire having been built by Hunslet & Co. Ltd in Leeds in 1938. However the bulk of its working life was spent at Earle's cement works at Hope in Derbyshire.

Once the top of the bank is reached the line straightens out along the site of the junction with the Great Northern Railway. For many years the first mile of trackbed out of Keighley had been shared with the GNR's Keighley to Bradford and Halifax branches. Very little evidence remains of the branch line and is unrecognisable due to the substantial tree growth of the intervening years.

In October 2012 the LMS Ivatt Class 4 2-6-0 No. 43106, a visitor from the Severn Valley Railway thunders through the trees as it leaves the 'straight'. This 1951 Doncaster-built locomotive is just one of the class that were considered to be among the ugliest British locomotives produced due to high positioning of the running plate which left a gap ahead of the cylinders. Hence the nickname 'Flying Pigs'.

Ingrow once boasted two stations. Ingrow East was on the now closed Great Northern Line with Ingrow West serving the Worth Valley Branch. When the society took over the line in 1961 the original building had suffered at the hands of vandals to the point that it was beyond restoration. Remarkably, twenty years later, a donation from a private individual responding to an appeal for funds to purchase a 'new' building resulted in the society being able to buy the former station building at Foulridge in Lancashire. It had been closed since 1959. The whole structure was dismantled, transported to Ingrow and rebuilt stone by stone! It re-opened in 1989. The station yard is home to two award winning transport museums. The Bahamas Locomotive Society occupies the former goods shed. This society is primarily dedicated to preserving in operational condition LMS 'Jubilee' Class No 45596 'Bahamas' but has also acquired additional locomotives including the famous ex-LNWR 'Coal Tank' No. 1054. At the far end of the yard is the excellent Museum of Rail Travel, home of the Vintage Carriages Trust mentioned earlier.

Opposite: *The final approach to the first station at Ingrow is still within the industrial belt around Keighley but pockets of stonewalled fields do begin to appear. Passing this paddock with a short works train is the KWVR's Taff Vale Tank. Taff Vale Railway Class O2 0-6-2T No. 85 was built for the TVR in 1899. This railway connected Cardiff and surrounding area with the coal fields to the north. No. 85 worked their steeply graded lines until the 1920s when it became surplus to requirements under the new Great Western Railway ownership. It was sold in 1929 and moved to the North East of England where it worked coal trains until displaced by diesel power in 1968. It arrived on KWVR metals in 1970. This picture dates from February 2008. In 2010 the locomotive was withdrawn from service and at the time of writing is nearing completion of a thorough overhaul.*

The line now passes through Ingrow Tunnel and used to emerge between tall mill buildings at the start of a gradient steepening to 1 in 56. Over the last few years redevelopment has transformed the former industrial landscape into one of new residential housing and flats. Sweeping round this curved section is another of the railway's home fleet. British Railways Standard Class 4MT 2-6-4T No. 80002 was built in Derby in 1952 and spent much of its working life in Scotland surviving beyond withdrawal in 1967 as it was retained by British Railways as a carriage-heating boiler at Cowlairs, Glasgow. It was purchased for preservation and moved to Yorkshire in 1969. Since this photograph was taken in 2011 the locomotive's boiler ticket has expired and it is currently a static display in the exhibition shed at Oxenhope.

The railway now leaves the urban environment behind as Damems is approached and here a new riverside park and walk has been created. On 2 March 2013 another Great Central Railway locomotive was hired in for a Gala. British Railways Class 2 2-6-0 No. 78019 provides a powerful exhaust as it passes close by the river. The KWVR has its own representative of these Class 2 locomotives in No. 78022 which is currently out of service but has recently undergone a thorough inspection to ascertain the amount of work necessary to get it back to full working order.

Damems Station is not only the smallest station on the line but also considered to be the smallest on British railways. It has one, one-coach-length platform and a station building that was originally a checker's office inside Keighley Goods Shed. The signalbox came from Earby Crossing on the Colne to Skipton line. Note the steps that show that the platform is set lower than is usual.

Just beyond the station is the passing loop which was constructed by volunteers in 1970. Completion allowed the railway to operate a two train service thus doubling the number of passengers that could be carried. The driver of this vintage train has just received the token that will allow him to proceed over the next section of the line all the way to the Oxenhope terminus. His charge is the Lancashire and Yorkshire Railway Class 25 'Ironclad' 0-6-0 No. 957. This Victorian locomotive emerged from the Beyer Peacock Works Manchester, in 1887 and survived until withdrawn from British Railways service in May 1959. The engine has a long list of film and television credits but is best known for its starring role in the feature film 'The Railway Children' for which it carried a green livery earning it the unofficial name of the 'Green Dragon'. This photograph was taken in the summer of 2010 when the loco-motive was nearing the end of its boiler ticket. It has since been withdrawn and awaits its ten yearly overhaul, on display at Oxenhope.

The line is now in open countryside as it winds its way hillside on the climb to Oakworth. Black 5 No. 45212 is a London, Midland & Scottish Railway Class 5 4-6-0 locomotive that was built in Newcastle in 1935. Its place in railway history was secured when it hauled the final steam-hauled revenue earning service for British Railways on 4 August 1968. The KWVR bought this locomotive directly from BR and it arrived on the line in October 1968. Since this photograph was taken in August 2011, 45212's boiler certificate has also expired. However, thanks to a ten year agreement with a Bury-based engineering company it is undergoing a major overhaul which when complete will see it operating main line specials in addition to some services on the KWVR.

Oakworth bank is one of the most popular locations on the line for railway photographers with locomotives having to work hard as they tackle the climb from a standing start at Damems loop. It must be noted that this location is just one of many viewpoints used in this book that are not available to the general public. It can only be accessed by members of the society in possession of a lineside pass and correctly attired with a hi-viz vest. Check the railway's website for membership details.

On 9 March 2014, London & North Eastern Railway Class K4 2-6-0 No. 61994 'The Great Marquess' a visitor for that weekend's Gala, took part in an early morning freight charter and for once the sun appeared on time!

Oakworth is the jewel in the Worth Valley Railway's crown. In so far as is possible the station is kept in its 1905-1914 condition with gas lighting to the platform and in the office and waiting room, classic enamel advertising signs and platform furniture of the period. Behind the station is the goods yard with weighbridge, goods shed, bay platform with a five ton crane still in place.

Built at Crewe in 1888 The London & North Western Railway 0-6-2 'Coal Tank' No. 1054, is looked after by the Bahamas Locomotive Society. In 2011 it emerged from an extensive overhaul which had been completed with support from the Heritage Lottery Fund. On 1 April 2012, in its BR Black livery and number (58926) it was photographed departing Oakworth in glorious spring sunshine.

At this point the railway passes close to extensive Vale Mill buildings at Mytholmes. Built around 1785 this was originally a spinning mill. An interesting feature is that a wing of the building spans both the River Worth and Mytholmes Lane. The latter was possibly a later development to provide access to the railway station when the line opened.

Passing the mill on a lovely September day in 2013 was Black 5 No. 45305 on an extended visit from its home base at the Great Central Railway.

Standard Tank No. 80002 passing the same location viewed from the lane beneath the mill on a cold 12 February 2011.

USA Transportation Corps Class S160 2-8-0 No. 5820, known to most as 'Big Jim', was built by Lima in Ohio for the USA army to aid the war effort. Its working life was spent in Poland. After withdrawal from active service it was preserved by the Polish Railway Museum before being purchased by the KWVR. It arrived in West Yorkshire in November 1977 entering service a year later. It was withdrawn in 1992 and eventually underwent a massive overhaul emerging from the works in February 2014. For its 'running-in' period it was temporarily painted in British Railways unlined black and carried the fictitious number 95820. To the relief of many by the time of this photograph (April 2014) 5820 had been returned to its authentic USA Transportation Corps grey livery.

At this point the line originally crossed the mill dam by a wooden trestle viaduct before curving around to the east of Penistone Hill. The route was diverted by the Midland Railway in 1892. The deviation saw the wooden structure replaced by a number of substantial bridges, the three arch Mytholmes Viaduct and Mytholmes Tunnel. The railway's unique WD No. 90733 leaves a perfect exhaust trail as it passes with an early morning freight on 2 March 2013.

Opposite: *Crossing the viaduct with another early freight train is No. 61994 'The Great Marquess'. The chimney in the background is all that is left of Lower Providence Mill.*

A classic vintage scene! The 1887-built Lancashire & Yorkshire locomotive No. 957 hauling a train that includes, as the two leading coaches, examples of stock from that same railway company. Immediately behind the tender is a L&YR 5 Compartment Third 6 fixed-wheel carriage dating from 1882. Behind that a 1910-built L&YR Hughes Taper-end Brake Third that contained 5 passenger compartments and one guard's compartment.

The approach to Mytholmes Tunnel as viewed from the Oakworth hillside on a cold crisp winter's day in December 2014.

The valley had a covering of snow as late as March in 2013. No. 80002 has just emerged from Mytholmes Tunnel and is rapidly approaching the next stop – Haworth.

Haworth Station was built to serve the famous village that was once home of the Brontë Sisters. With its goods yard, it is the largest station on the line and has been the headquarters of the preservation society from its inception. Whilst it is similar in style to the other KWVR stations and externally retains an air of times past, the internal arrangement has been altered to reflect the necessary commercial activities of the railway. The former waiting room has long been converted to a shop and more recently a new sympathetically designed toilet block has been constructed.

The railway's locomotive shed and workshops are based around the former goods shed and yard a short distance from the station. The old shed is the perfect backcloth for night-time photography of the locomotives at rest. During the October 2012 Gala the locomotives were lined up under floodlighting for that very purpose.

Just south of Haworth the line runs parallel to Bridgehouse Beck. Withdrawn in 1987, 4F No. 43924 had only just returned to service following overhaul at the time of this special chartered freight train – 22 September 2011.

Just before the 'Coal Tank' ended its working days at Pontypool in 1958 it had worked the last train on the Abergavenny to Merthyr Line with 0-8-0 locomotive No. 49121. In 2012 the visit of LNWR Class G2 0-8-0 (Super 'D') No. 49395 was an opportunity not to be missed so a re-enactment of that final Stephenson Locomotive Society special was run on a very cold February morning. No. 43935 was re-numbered for the occasion.

Keeping with the Welsh theme at the same location, approaching 'top field', in the summer of 2007 with the Taff Vale Tank in charge of passenger services.

The 'top field', as named by railway photographers, is an attractive stretch of the line midway between Haworth and Oxenhope and accessible via public footpaths. In February 2011 the unusual sight of double-headed Black 5s roaring up the valley was a highlight of the Winter Gala. Privately owned No. 44767 'George Stephenson' and the East Lancashire Railway's No. 44871 stole the show with their powerful performances.

The 4F and its three suburban coaches create a branch line scene that epitomises the Worth Valley Railway.

From the height of summer to the depths of winter. The same location viewed from the footpath on the other side of the tracks. Black 5 No. 45305 and its Santa Special train draw the attention of a young family stretching their legs.

British Railways Standard Class 4MT 4-6-0 No. 75078 was, for many years, a stalwart of the railway, before withdrawal for a heavy overhaul in the late nineties. Built at Swindon in 1956 it spent much of its working life based at Basingstoke until 1963 when it was transferred to Nine Elms in London. Two years later Eastleigh became the locomotive's final home as in July 1966 it was pulled out of service and sold to the Woodhams' Scrapyard in South Wales. This locomotive was chosen for purchase by the Standard 4 Preservation Society and it was moved to the KWVR in June 1972, entering service in 1977. Following a further overhaul, it returned to traffic in February 2015, temporarily in an unlined black livery, and will hopefully now see many years of action on Worth Valley rails.

After the 'straight' at top field the line curves gently passing through a wooded area on the final approach to the terminus at Oxenhope.

After a twenty-five-year restoration, August 2014 saw the long awaited return to steam of an old favourite – British Railways, Bulleid West Country Pacific 4-6-2 No. 34092 'City of Wells'. Built in 1949 it saw regular use on prestigious trains such as the 'Golden Arrow' boat train between London and Dover. The locomotive was sold to the Woodham Brothers' South Wales scrapyard on withdrawal in 1964 and languished there until rescued by a group of individuals in 1971 who brought it to the Worth Valley in 1971. It worked the line for ten years from 1979 until 1989. For twelve months when first built, the engine was given the name 'Wells' and that is the name it was carrying on 27 February 2015.

The journey terminates at Oxenhope Station located in a typical Pennine village in the shadow of the surrounding moors. The adjacent goods shed is used for the restoration and servicing of the passenger carriages and goods stock. Opposite the station entrance is the three road Exhibition Shed that houses locomotives that are out of traffic long term and little used coaching stock. This is open to the public. To the east of the station is an open-sided covered shed where the operational carriage fleet is stored, protected from the worst of the Pennine weather.

The Keighley & Worth Valley Railway has led the way in preservation with its late 1950s'/early 1960s' house style so clearly depicted with period totems, handbills and posters, stations warmed by coal fires, lit by gas, adorned with hanging baskets and staffed by volunteers whose attire is complete with red uniform ties. The railway is run by qualified volunteers and has operated every weekend for over four decades. Long may it continue.

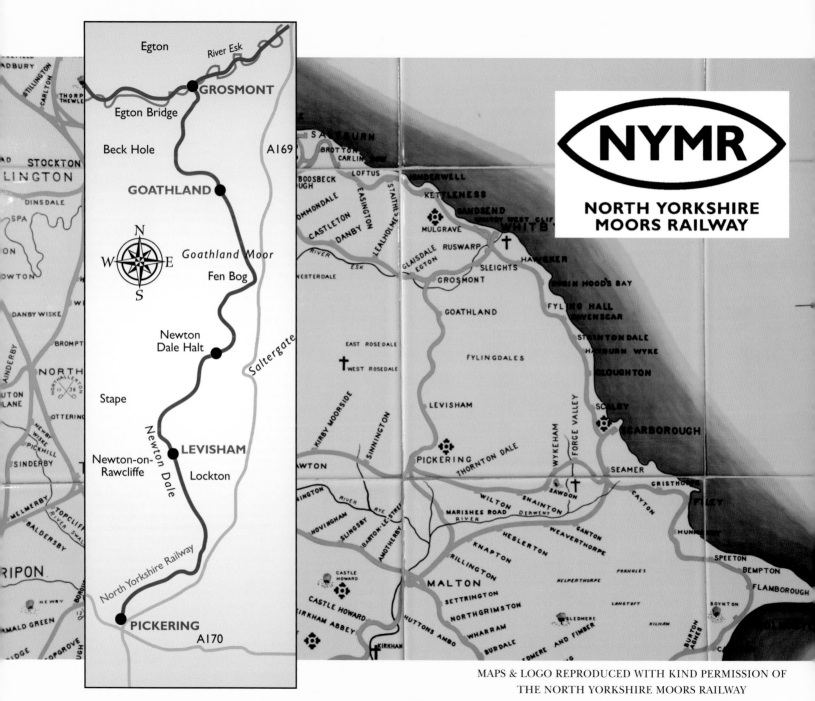

NYMR

NORTH YORKSHIRE
MOORS RAILWAY

The North Yorkshire Moors Railway

The North Yorkshire Moors Railway, which dates from the earliest days of railway building, runs for 24 miles from the seaside at Whitby through the North Yorkshire Moors National Park to the market town of Pickering. The first stage opened in 1835 and linked Whitby with Grosmont, advancing to Pickering the following year. The Whitby to Pickering Railway was initially operated throughout by horse-drawn carriages except for a rope-worked incline between Beckhole and Goathland.

In 1845 the York and North Midland Railway (Y&NM) built a railway from York to Scarborough including a link to Pickering. One year later steam locomotives were introduced to work on the section to Levisham from the south and to Whitby in 1847. The route was now double tracked creating a bottleneck at the incline where it was not possible to use locomotives, a major hold up to services on the route.

In 1854 the Y&NM was amalgamated into the North Eastern Railway (NER) who completed the railway line from Middlesborough to Whitby linking with the old Whitby & Pickering Railway at Grosmont. They also reconstructed the route between Grosmont and the summit of the line at Fen Bog. Known as the 'deviation', this new route was opened in 1865, and included the replacement of the incline allowing locomotives to work the full length of the line for the first time.

For over ninety years the railway settled down to the routine business of moving people and goods to and from Whitby until traffic began to decline in the 1930s as the 'Depression' greatly reduced the industrial demand for the shipment of goods. Post war, the demise continued across Britain's railways to the point that the 1963 'Beeching Report' proposed the closure of all the railway routes into Whitby. Intense public pressure managed to save the Esk Valley line from Whitby to Middlesborough but all other routes were closed. The final British Railway's operated train over the route ran on 6 March 1965 and was hauled by LNER K4 No. 3442 'The Great Marquess' and LNER K1 No. 62005.

However a group of enthusiasts were keen for the railway not to become just a memory and established a preservation society in 1967 with the aim of reopening the line for the benefit of the community. Track lifting of the route was postponed to allow the preservationists time to develop a proposal for the route. In April 1968 British Railways agreed to leave a single track in place from Grosmont to Ellerbeck, although, as it happens, a single line was left throughout. Late that year the first items of rolling stock began to arrive on the railway and over the next few years the preservation society accumulated numerous locomotives and coaching stock. They also obtained the necessary Light Railway Order.

On 1st May 1973 the Duchess of Kent attended the official opening of the railway although trains would not run regularly into Pickering Station until 1975 as, at the time, the site was proposed to be used for a car park!

Since then the railway has gone from strength to strength and from 2007 has also been able to operate regular services from Grosmont into Whitby itself. Here the station has seen Platform 2 reinstated for the sole use of NYMR trains.

The line now carries around 300,000 passengers a year and boasts being the country's most popular heritage line. So jump onboard and enjoy a journey down the line to savour the magnificent achievements of the preservation society and the dramatic North Yorkshire scenery enjoyed by thousands of passengers each year.

Rooted in the seventh Century with the construction of the Abbey, Whitby was famous for the production of alum for the leather and medicine industries. Later the town offered an ideal port for whaling, fishing and boat building. However, despite this it was not until 1759 that the first turnpike road was constructed to Pickering. Therefore as the railway boom began it was a natural target for railway developers resulting in four railway routes to the town being constructed. These radiated out from Whitby to the north, south and west but all were threatened with closure in the 1960s. Following local pressure the direct line to Middlesbrough was saved but the line to Pickering, often regarded as the main line, was closed opening the door for preservation. Since 2005 the NYMR has operated a steam service to Whitby which expanded in 2014 following the opening of a second platform at the station for NYMR service use.

On 4 June 2014, No. 75029 'The Green Knight' powers away from Whitby with the ruins of the eleventh-century Abbey prominent on the hillside.

Grosmont Station sits at the heart of the village with a level crossing which allows the line to cross the main road. These views taken in 2015 show the station's blue and cream colour scheme which represents the 1950s' period when the railway was under the control of the Eastern Region of British Railways. The colours are actually monsoon blue, gardenia and tangerine. The former two were used in part of the promotion of the route as a line to the seaside with the colours representing the sea and sand. Tangerine is used for the signs as it was across the entire North Eastern Region. Whilst the stone buildings are original, the wooden buildings on Platform 1 come from Sleights Station which lies between here and Whitby on the Esk Valley line. In the right hand photo the railway's flagship engine, LNER A4 'Sir Nigel Gresley' awaits departure.

May 2015 saw the first ever 'Tour de Yorkshire' cycle race when the world's elite cyclists compete over a three-day race around the county. On 1 May the race passed through Grosmont and was saluted by Black 5s 45407 'The Lancashire Fusilier' and 44871 standing alongside 'Sir Nigel Gresley', blowing their whistles as the riders passed.

Grosmont is also the home to the railway's engineering base which features the only coal hopper on any preserved line in Britain. These views show the engines on shed preparing for the day's activities and the left-hand view clearly shows the tower with No. 75029 awaiting coaling beneath.

Soon after passing the sheds the line separates from the 1836 route and starts the climb onto the Moors. LNER B1 No. 61264 puts on a display of power with a Breakdown Crane charter in November 2013. The effort is not for show as this crane weighs approximately 200 tonnes and provides a stern test for an engine on this demanding railway.

The remote hamlet of Esk Valley is passed by former LNER K4 class No. 61994 'The Great Marquess' in May 2015 at the start of the long ascent to Goathland. This engine is the only survivor of a class of 6 which were especially designed for use on the West Highland main line and extension in Scotland. The engine is therefore ideal for the NYMR with its steep climbs and sharp curves.

The train is on the 'deviation' although a short section of the original route remained to Esk Valley until 1951. The route of this short branch was between the white cottage and the stone buildings and a small section can be seen in the lower right centre of the photo. This branch had been retained to serve Esk Valley Cottages which, until 1951, were not served by any road and were only connected after the residents self-funded its construction.

The changing of the season is very pronounced on the moors. The previous page's spring has given way to autumn in this view of visiting Manor Class No. 7822 'Foxcote Manor', on loan from the Llangollen Railway, heading south with an afternoon train during the 2011 October Steam Gala.

A feature of NYMR Galas are freight trains which tend to operate between Grosmont and Goathland. These freights are often used on early morning charters where a group of photographers pay for the train to run before the timetabled services so that they can take photographs in locations of their choosing. On May 12 2012 Southern Region S15 class No. 825 was the engine of choice for the charter and is captured powering past Green End.

For the May 2012 Gala the NYMR hired in two main-line engines from the Jeremy Hosking's stable of regular performers on the national network. Powering through Beckhole is one of these visitors, namely BR Standard No. 70000 'Britannia'. Following the nationalisation of the 'Big Four' railway companies (The Great Western, Southern, London & North Eastern and London Midland & Scottish) in 1948, the newly formed British Railways developed a fleet of standard designs. No. 70000 was the first of 999 engines built to these designs and the North Yorkshire Moors is home to a number of engines from this 'standard' family including No. 75029 'The Green Knight' seen on shed earlier.

A little further up the climb Black 5 No. 44767 'George Stephenson', named during preservation in honour of the 'Father of the Railways', tackles the gradient at the head of 'The Moorlander' dining train on 1 October 2011. The Black 5s were once the most numerous type of engine in Britain, with 842 built in total. No. 44767 was unique in being the only member of the class fitted with Stephenson Link House motion. It is now based on the North Norfolk Railway but makes occasional visits elsewhere.

It is not only large tender engines that operate on the NYMR. BR Standard Class 4 Tank No. 80072 makes a surefooted ascent near Thomason Foss. On this section the railway crosses Eller Beck three times in quick succession.

This engine, another member of the BR standard classes, spent two years on loan to the NYMR from the Llangollen Railway between 2011 and 2012. The railway's own standard tank, No. 80135, is at the time of writing undergoing an overhaul to return it to service.

BR Eastern Region K1 Class No. 62005 crosses Water Ark Bridge on 6 May 2013 during another Spring Gala. This engine was built by British Railways in 1949 and is one of four owned by the North Eastern Locomotive Preservation Group (NELPG) all of which are based on the railway. Whilst well suited to the line's gradients 62005 spends much of the year hauling 'The Jacobite', the popular daily steam train between Fort William and Mallaig in the West Highlands of Scotland.

Showing once again how the moorland scenery changes throughout the year. Q6 Class No. 63395, another of the four NELPG owned engines, heads a freight train to Goathland on 17 October 2009. 63395 arrived on the line in 1970 and was the first main line engine to be based on the railway. The Q6 Class, constructed to haul freight, were employed extensively in the North East of England. It is therefore very fitting that the sole surviving member of the class is based on the North Yorkshire Moors Railway.

Former London and North Western Railway Class G2a locomotives were known as known as Super Ds. The preserved example, No. 49395, canters through Thomason Foss at the head of a goods train on October 1 2010. This engine is owned by the National Railway Museum and was returned to service by the efforts of the 'celebrity' enthusiast, Pete Waterman. However, at the time of writing, the locomotive is awaiting overhaul once again.

Another photo taken on a morning freight charter sees visiting Manor No. 7822 'Foxcote Manor' blast under the road bridge on the approach to Darnholm.

Overlooking the tight curve at Darnholm is a very popular spot for photographers with engines working hard on the 1 in 49 gradient to Goathland. These views show how the location changes throughout the year. Left: *Resident Black 5 No. 45428 brings a spring service onto the curve in May 2010,* top right: *No. 825 captured in an unusual wide view in May 2012 and finally* bottom right: *in the height of summer USA Transport Corps S160 No. 6046, a sister engine to No. 5820 seen earlier on the KWVR, visiting from the Churnet Valley Railway blackens the skies on 3 August 2013.*

However, the location is at its most colourful in autumn when the ferns and trees turn golden. On 1 October 2011, just after the sun has risen over the hillside, No. 7822 'Foxcote Manor' storms by at the head of another morning charter freight train.

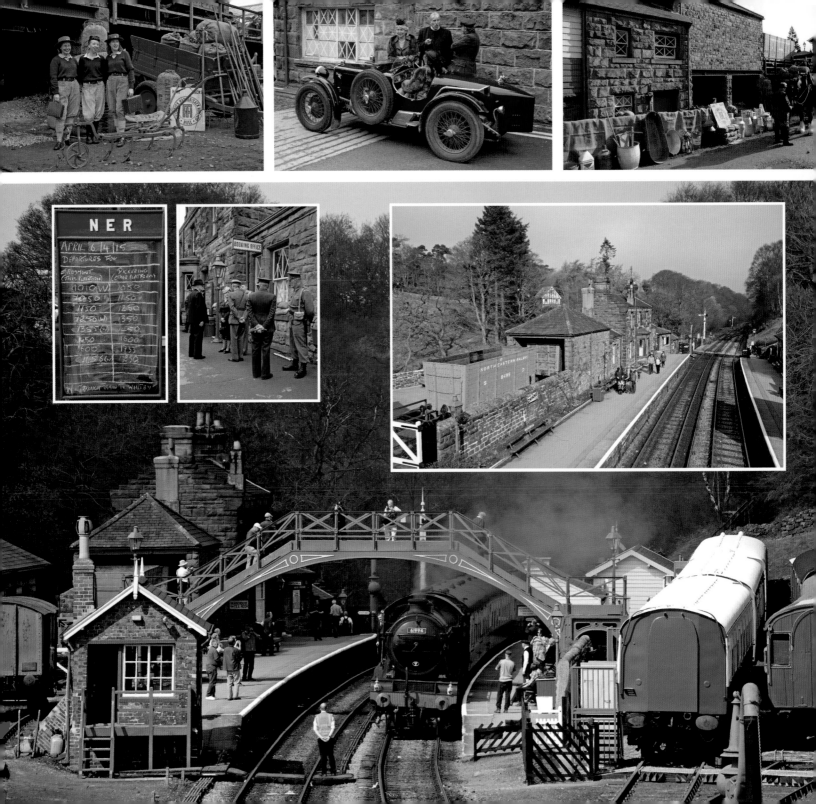

NER

APRIL 6 14 15

DEPARTURES FOR

GROSMONT (THIS PLATFORM)	PICKERING (OTHER PLATFORM)
1010 (W)	1050
1250 (C)	1150
1150	1250
1250 (W)	1350
1355 (C)	1450
1450	1600
1500	1755
1756 (W)	1850

(W) THROUGH TRAIN TO WHITBY

BOOKING OFFICE

NORTH EASTERN RAILWAY

61994

On loan from the Midland Railway Centre, Butterley in Derbyshire and a long way from its native Somerset and Dorset Railway for which it was constructed is 7F No. 53809. In October 2009 it was photographed hauling a freight train away from Goathland. The area to the right beyond the signal used to house the Whinestone Quarry crushing buildings. These were served by horse-drawn tramways, the route of which can still be traced when walking on the hillside.

Opposite: Goathland Station will be familiar to many as 'Aidensfield' from the Television series 'Heartbeat' but more recently has become famous as 'Hogsmeade' Station in the Harry Potter films. The railway was used to film some of the scenes of the 'Hogwarts Express' in the countryside. This is the newest station on the railway, being built as part of the deviation works, the original railway being further up the hill. Goathland station is kept in the copper and beech colour scheme of the NER as it would have looked in the 1920s. The station takes a leading role in many events held on the railway and these photos are taken during one of 1940s' weekends during which the station and yard are transported back to the forties to commemorate those who served their country at this time.

Another view of No. 75029. As the mist clears on 7 December 2008 the Swindon-built engine barks away from Goathland through the snow.

The third of the four NELPG-owned engines (the fourth is currently out of service and is under overhaul) class J72 No. 69023 'Joem' shunts the freight at Goathland on 12 May 2012. This locomotive is too small for the regular service at the railway but often runs at Galas on local trains and freights spending the rest of the year on hire to other preserved railways.

The culmination of eighteen years of work by the 'A1 Steam Locomotive Trust' to fill a gap in the preserved fleet of front line LNER express engines, saw new-build LNER A1 'Tornado' enter service in 2008. The engine has been a regular visitor to the NYMR in the years since and is captured on 2 October 2010 heading out onto the moors with the LNER teak set of coaches – the 'Teak train'.

Opposite, top: *Southern Railway Schools Class No. 30926 'Repton' is a member of the most powerful 4-4-0 engines ever built in the UK and has been seen much use on the railway since it was repatriated from the USA in 1989. Although under overhaul at the time of writing, this view dating from May 2010 sees the engine steaming across the moorland landscape at Abbots House.*

Opposite, bottom: *Standard Tank No. 80072 heads through Moorgates in June 2012. The triangle building on the horizon is RAF Fylingdales which was famous for having three large golf-ball-shaped buildings which dominated the scene until the mid 1990s.*

The last British Railway's train from 1965 was re-enacted in 2007 when K4 'The Great Marquess' led K1 No. 62005 through Moorgates on a beautiful autumn evening. In the foreground can be seen the formation of the original Whitby and Pickering Railway which meets the 1865 deviation route at Moorgates.

LNER K4 'The Great Marquess' is a regular visitor to the railway and is captured on a sunny 1 May 2015 heading a spring service to Pickering with the abandoned formation symbolically in shadow in 150th anniversary year of the deviation opening in 1865.

No trip down the North Yorkshire Moors Railway would be complete without seeing the landscape covered in snow. S15 No. 825 canters through a winter landscape on 7 December 2008 at the head of 'The Moorlander' dining train.

On 3 July 1938 LNER A4 No. 4468 'Mallard' set the world steam speed record at 126mph on Stoke Bank in Lincolnshire and is now preserved as a static exhibit in York at the National Railway Museum. Five other members of the class have been preserved. Two in museums in North America, the remaining three are currently in full working order and are regular performers across Britain. Here the second Jeremy Hosking's-owned engine visiting for the May 2012 Gala, No. 4464 'Bittern' wearing the Garter Blue livery of the London and North Eastern Railway sprints through Moorgates with the matching train of LNER wooden-bodied teak coaches recreating a scene from the East Coast Main Line during the 1930s.

Returning to 3 August 2013 and the summer greens see B1 No. 61264, running as scrapped classmate No. 61002 'Impala' passing the point at which the original line and the 1865 route meet. The original track bed enters on the middle left of the photograph and meets the new line bottom right.

BR Standard 9F No. 92214 at Moorgates in spring evening sunshine on 5 May 2012. This train is at the same point as the B1 in the previous photo but before the summer growth of ferns gets hold, meaning that the old formation is much clearer running diagonally from the bottom right to the centre. Since this was taken this 9F has been sold by its owner to a member of the Great Central Railway in Leicestershire and now resides on that railway.

Black 5 No. 45428 'Eric Treacy', another one of Sir William Stanier's celebrated Black 5s, leads the first train of a new year through Moorgates on 1 January 2013. This engine, unlike 45407, 44767 and 44871 seen elsewhere in this section, is owned by and is permanently based on the North Yorkshire Moors Railway.

A member of a class of engine that was regularly used on the line during the British Railways era, namely the LNER B1. This example, No. 61264, owned by the Thompson B1 Society is currently based on the railway. At the head of a Matt Fisher charter on 12 November 2013 the engine brings a breakdown crane through Ellerbeck.

The A169 Whitby road rises over the distant hills as an NYMR service steams over Fen Bog. This area of upland is a designated Site of Special Scientific Interest (SSSI) and is known to contain over 300 plant species. The bog, which is up to 12m deep, provided a significant challenge to the railway builders which necessitated the laying of wattle fences and heather-stuffed fleeces to carry the railway over it. To this day the bog rises and falls depending on the amount of water within and the railway does the same!

Another view of the 13 November Crane charter, after the loco had been turned on the Pickering turntable, sees No. 61264 ambling round the curve across the bog.

The bare slopes of Northdale show that this is a spring view of BR Standard No. 76079 passing Killing Nab Scar on 6 April 2015. This engine, built at Horwich in 1957, served British Railways until 1967 when withdrawn. One of four members of the class to be preserved, 76079 has been based on the Llangollen Railway and East Lancashire Railway during the preservation era and also saw a period of operation on the main line. However, in 2009 the engine was bought by the North Yorkshire Moors Railway and is now based there.

Northdale and Newtondale are thought to have been carved out by a melting glacier at the end of the last ice age when a surge of water cascaded across North Yorkshire following the collapse of an ice dam that was holding back the meltwater.

Deep in Northdale No. 61264 battles up the 1 in 54 climb near Carters House in the last light of the day.

Levisham Station is preserved in the condition in which it is likely to have appeared in 1912 during NER ownership. The village of Levisham is actually over a mile away and 90m above the valley bottom where the railway runs. This is an ideal location to get off the train to explore the numerous walks through the woods and onto the moors, that start from here.

BR standard No. 76079 restarts a train from Levisham Station beneath Howlgate Knab on 24 April 2015. The station buildings can be seen on the right and this photograph gives a hint towards the isolated location in which the station resides.

'The Green Knight' sprints away from Levisham on the afternoon of 6 April 2015. This view of the engine shows off the smart BR lined green livery which marks this locomotive out as a former British Railways Western Region example.

No. 76079 continues the journey through Newtondale. Whilst the railway was a main line when part of the national network and double track throughout from the 1860s the section between Levisham and Pickering (New Bridge) was reduced to a single track in 1916 to help with the war effort. This second line was never replaced.

A little way down the valley from Levisham is a collection of cottages at Farwath. Their gardens offer this view (taken with the owner's permission) of approaching trains. In this scene, from 3 May 2009, LNER A4 'Sir Nigel Gresley', built in 1937 as the 100th Gresley Pacific and named in the designer's honour, carrying the striking Express Blue livery of British Railways, drifts by with another 'The Moorlander' dining train. Ambling along a preserved railway at a maximum 25mph is very different to the intent for the engine when the class were constructed. They were built for the express services on the East Coast Main line. As previously noted LNER A4 'Mallard' holds the world steam record. Not to be outdone however 'Sir Nigel Gresley' holds the post war record of 112mph achieved on 23 May 1959. This feat was achieved at Stoke Bank, the same place as the 'Mallard' undertaking.

The tight meanders of Pickering Beck as its flows down Newtondale can clearly be seen in this view of a Pickering-bound 'Santa Special' train heading away from Farwath on 7 December 2008, with Black 5 No. 45212 at its head. The steam trail hangs long in the air, a clear sign of cold air on a day where temperatures didn't rise above -7°C.

Coasting to a standstill at Pickering Station is Black 5 No. 45407 'The Lancashire Fusilier' which has conquered the climbs of the North Yorkshire Moors Railway and arrived at the end of the line on 24 April 2015. The station site at Pickering had been earmarked for a car park when the railway originally closed in 1965 but thankfully was saved for the preserved railway. The station building dates from 1845 but lost its overall roof in 1952. It was a long held ambition of the preservation group to reinstate it and the dream was realised in 2011 when the structure was rebuilt with assistance from the Heritage Lottery Fund. This gives the railway a superb crowning glory to complete the LNER 1930s' look of the station.

Various views taken of Pickering Station which show the roof off to good effect. The station is complete with all manner of 'station furniture' which enhance the scene. Some of these items have been collected from elsewhere such as the footbridge from Tyneside and the buildings near the footbridge from Whitby. The train shed exudes atmosphere after dark as in this view of No. 61994 'The Great Marquess' awaiting to run round its train. Before 1965 when the line closed the railway extended away into the distance to Rillington Junction on the York to Scarborough Railway.

Journey's end on the NYMR sees Black 5 No. 44871 at rest after hauling an evening 'The Moorlander' dining train. After forty-eight years as a preservation society and forty-three years running trains, the North Yorkshire Moors Preservation Society can be justly proud of their achievements and long may they continue.

The Settle to Carlisle Railway

The Settle to Carlisle Railway was borne out of the desire of the Midland Railway to have its own direct link to Scotland. It totals 73 miles in length and was constructed in the 1870s across some of the bleakest of terrains, through the remote but scenic region of the Yorkshire Dales and Northern Pennines. The 14 mile long section within Yorkshire runs from just south of Settle to just north of the world-famous Ribblehead Viaduct. It was the alleged terminally poor condition of this viaduct that formed the basis for British Rail to seek closure of the line in the early 1980s. The story of the ultimately successful campaign to prevent this is well documented. Suffice to say that that the consolidated efforts of enthusiasts and local residents, led by the Friends of the Settle to Carlisle Railway, were rewarded when, in 1989, British Rail were finally refused permission to close it.

Repairs were then carried out and since then the line has gone from strength to strength with regular passenger services supplemented with the return of freight traffic transporting coal and gypsum.

The line's attraction for tourists has seen an ever increasing number of steam-hauled railtours pass along it giving passengers unrivalled views of the northern hills.

MAPS & LOGO IMAGES COURTESY OF SCRDC
(www.settle-carlisle.co.uk)

Right: Throughout the summer 'The Fellsman' railtour runs Lancaster – Preston – Settle – Carlisle and return. On 18 July 2012 8F No. 48151 was in charge and is seen drifting down towards Settle Junction where the S&C joins the Leeds to Carnforth line.

Below: On 21 March 2015 LMS Jubilee No. 45690 'Leander' climbs away from the junction with the 'Cumbrian Jubilee' excursion. This tour had started in Birmingham with diesel haulage to Hellifield where 'Leander' took over for the run along the S&C to Carlisle and later back to Carnforth via the West Coast Main Line.

'The Highlands & Islands Explorer' in May 2014 was a nine day railtour which travelled the length and breadth of the country. It was predominantly steam hauled and took in the most scenic railway routes in mainland Britain. The Settle to Carlisle leg was double-headed by Black 5s No. 44871 and 45407 'The Lancashire Fusilier'. Here they have just passed through Settle Station and are approaching Langcliffe.

On 27 July 2013 that day's 'Cumbrian Mountain Express' passes Langliffe in the capable hands of LMS Princess Coronation Class 4-6-2 Pacific No. 46233 'Duchess of Sutherland'. The 'Duchesses' were a class of express passenger locomotives designed by William Stanier for the London, Midland and Scottish Railway's West Coast Main Line from London to Glasgow.

3 July 2010. The unique British Railways Standard Class 8 4-6-2 Pacific No. 71000 'Duke of Gloucester' with the multi-coloured stock of 'The Cumbrian Coast Explorer' approaches, then crosses Helwith Bridge as it travels south. Pen y Ghent, one of the Yorkshire Three Peaks, forms the background to the view of the bridge.

Getting into its stride, just south of Selside, is BR Standard Class 7 4-6-2 Pacific No. 70000 'Britannia' with a full rake of matching crimson and cream coaching stock for the 'Cumbrian Mountain Express' on 3 March 2012. Again Pen y Ghent dominates the landscape. (The cab top had been painted white for recent Royal Train duties.)

For many years another regular railtour has been 'The Waverley' which runs from York to Carlisle and return. In the soft evening sunlight of 29 August 2010 LMS Royal Scot Class 4-6-0 No. 46115 'Scots Guardsman' cruises through Selside with the return working.

On 10 March 2012 the 'Shap, Settle and Carlisle' railtour (Carnforth-Shap-Carlisle-Settle-Crewe) started out being double-headed by locomotives LMS Princess Royal Class No. 46201 'Princess Elizabeth' and Great Western Railway 4073 Class 4-6-0 No. 5043 'Earl of Mount Edgecumbe'. This imaginative pairing was separated at Carlisle when the 'Princess' was 'stopped' having failed. This left the GWR locomotive to tackle the Settle to Carlisle on its own which it seemed to do with ease and presented onlookers with this some-what rare view of a Great Western train in the heart of the Northern Fells, on the renowned Ribblehead Viaduct.

Sunset at Ribblehead. The classic streamlined profile of LNER Class A4 No. 60009 'Union of South Africa' is silhouetted against the setting sun as it heads south with the 'Winter Cumbrian Mountain Express' on the 2 February 2013.

Thanks to the efforts of the campaign group that took on the might of British Rail and thwarted their attempts to close the Settle to Carlisle line back in the 1980s, evocative nostalgic scenes such as this can still be created today and hopefully for many years to come.